DOG BITES!

canine cuisine

Rick & Martha Reynolds

Illustrations by

Rick Reynolds

BERKLEY BOOKS, NEW YORK

DOG BITES!

canine cuisine

**A Berkley Book / published by arrangement with
Wieser & Wieser, Inc.**

PRINTING HISTORY
Berkley trade paperback edition / November 1992

Book design and mechanicals by
Media Dynamics
Armonk, New York 10504

ISBN: 0-425-13511-X

A BERKLEY BOOK ® TM 757,375

Berkley Books are published by
The Berkley Publishing Group,
200 Madison Avenue, New York, New York 10016.
The name **"BERKLEY"** and the **"B"** logo
are trademarks belonging to Berkley Publishing Corporation.

PRINTED IN THE UNITED STATES OF AMERICA

10   9   8   7   6   5   4   3   2   1

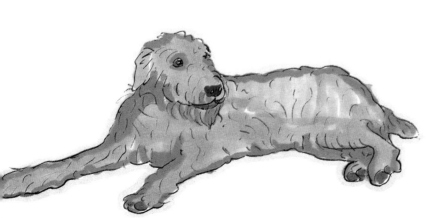

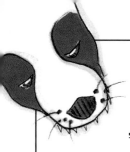

Contents

1 THE WAY TO A DOG'S

A Foreword

Our dog Bo loves to go wherever we go and eat whatever we eat. We try to include him in our activities and offer him a variety of foods that add zest and nutrition to his diet. No one has ever proven that dogs need variety. Bo would argue that no one has ever proven that people need variety either. In our family "variety is the spice of life" and that's what this book is all about.

It is understandable that as humans we are interested in menu variety. After all, when you're at the top of the food chain you have a lot of choice in what you eat. Those below us on the food chain arguably spend less time thinking about choice and more time worrying about becoming someone else's meal. All animals, humans included, can be content with a monotonous diet, as long as their exposure to other foods is limited. My friend Johnny eats hamburgers three times a day, seven days a week. He seems happy. His dog won't roll over for carrots like mine will. His dog doesn't know what carrots are. Instead, Johnny's dog is quite content getting hamburger tidbits from time to time.

HEART

Since dogs can't be interviewed, many people conclude that routine is something they desire. It is a human prejudice to think that we are the only species capable of appreciating the five senses we all share, that only our experiences are relevant.

Dogs have a sense of smell one million times greater than our own. Only eels can smell better, but they're hard to warm up to. One only has to remember their last head cold to be reminded of how critical smell is to taste. Compared with our dogs, we miss the world's subtle smells; it's as if we were walking around with clothespins on our noses.

It is impossible to document with any precision how our canine friends perceive flavor. There is evidence that in the wild, dogs— as well as their cousins the fox, wolf, coyote and hyena — will pass up an older carcass for a newer one. Dogs are often attracted to things we consider foul-smelling. But beauty is in the nose of the beholder;

after all, human connoisseurs crave many foods that are teeming with live cultures, such as cheese, yogurt, bread and wine.

That aside, dogs certainly do communicate pleasure when eating foods they like. After wolfing down a treat, Bo will point his nose skyward and close his eyes as if to say "mmm."

Though creatures of habit to some extent, dogs, like us, will often try new foods if they have the chance. An old college friend of mine lost his dog in an area surrounded by orchards. Two months later, after all hope was lost, word of his dog came in through the network of migrant workers. The dog was living in the orchards eating apples and had actually put on a few pounds. Long after their reunion, apples were the snack of choice for both of them.

Hearing, too, is far more advanced in dogs. Bo can hear a small, nocturnal animal tiptoeing in the woods outside our house. Through thick walls and storm windows, a howling wind and my awful snoring, he can detect the movement of tiny feet a hundred yards away. In his private acoustical world, he can hear things he cannot share with me.

Dogs' eyesight is not nearly as acute as their other senses and is poor compared with ours. However, in the absence of smell, movement, and sound, dogs interpret and translate visual symbols.

Once we brought home a life-sized cement figure of a West Highland White Terrier for the garden. Bo ran up to it, wagging his tail, and immediately headed for the posterior for a sniff. Disappointed, Bo circled his inanimate double, barking and pouncing.

Bo also watches television. My friend Joe says he's only following the movement — the lights and darks — the flickering. But then how does one explain Bo's love of animal shows? When we watch old videos of Wild Kingdom, his attention span is longer than mine. When the predator chases the prey across the screen, Bo crouches down, trembling — his eyes following every movement. Naturally, Bo gets bored when Marlin Perkins abruptly segues from the hazards of the wild to your family's insurance needs. That's when we all head for a snack.

Bo looks "out" the TV screen like he looks out the window. This is not to suggest that he follows soap operas and sitcoms, and some would argue that this is to his credit. Rather, Bo prefers catching glimpses of relevant programs like the Westminster Dog Show or old Lassie movies. When a TV dog barks,

Bo is the only one in the room who knows what it means. If the barking continues, mayhem breaks out.

We are convinced that dogs are especially suited to enjoy their senses. Even their sense of touch is heightened. When Bo and I are in a room, he will gravitate toward me. Eventually he will lean against my leg to express his presence, his connection. When his ears are stroked, he squints his eyes, drifting in and out of the dream state. He lifts his paw onto my hand and licks the air. Our dog friends clearly live in the realm of the senses.

When we humans begin to lose our bias, we realize the world was not made exclusively for us. Flowers were not designed so beautifully to appeal to our eyes or for our gratification. Indeed, they preceded us by many millions of years. Rather, they were designed to appeal to the birds and the bees, who in turn, ensure the flowers' survival. Thankfully, we can all appreciate the variety that surrounds us.

Perhaps the most gratifying aspect about the human experience is that we tend to enjoy most the time we share with others, and our dogs seem to be in total harmony with that concept. In fact, dogs are especially attuned to the art of companionship, devotion and the desire to please.

The way to a dog's heart then is through his senses, not just through his stomach. This book is about cooking for your dog and about nurturing your relationship. It is about interacting with another species and, in the process, discovering something nice about your own.

2 IN THE BELLY OF THE

An Introduction to the Recipes

L ong before political action committees and insider trading had any relevance to us, we were cutting our own under-the-table deals. Before the age of five, we made secret trades at considerable risk— deals where the currency was vegetables and the trading partners our family dogs, who in exchange sat poker-faced, offering complete confidentiality. Little did we know that these under-the-table deals benefited our pet's nutrition at the expense of our own.

Now we're grown up, eating our own vegetables and raising our own dog. It was no surprise that Bo liked vegetables as much as our old family dogs did, but we didn't expect such enthusiasm. All we have to do is hold up the carrot peeler, and Bo will come running. The sound of someone crunching into a piece of celery or an apple will draw Bo away from whatever he's doing. This isn't to say that Bo doesn't also love the more conventional dog treats like liver biscuits or leftover lamb. He

BEAST

seems to enjoy and thrive on the variety in his diet.

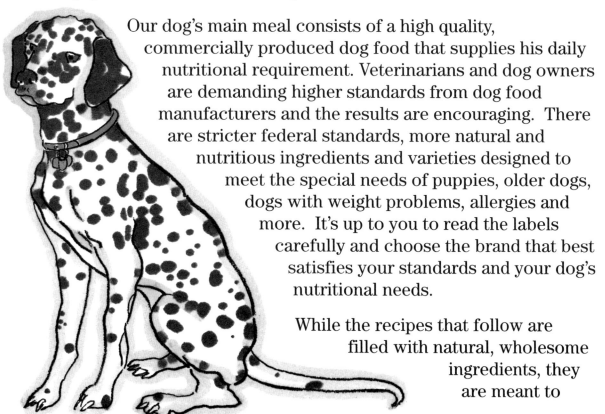

Our dog's main meal consists of a high quality, commercially produced dog food that supplies his daily nutritional requirement. Veterinarians and dog owners are demanding higher standards from dog food manufacturers and the results are encouraging. There are stricter federal standards, more natural and nutritious ingredients and varieties designed to meet the special needs of puppies, older dogs, dogs with weight problems, allergies and more. It's up to you to read the labels carefully and choose the brand that best satisfies your standards and your dog's nutritional needs.

While the recipes that follow are filled with natural, wholesome ingredients, they are meant to supplement the daily meal, not replace it. These treats have been tested by a variety of canine consultants and were enthusiastically received. But dogs, like people, have different preferences and varying abilities to digest certain foods. Bo happens to love carrots and apples. But he won't go near oranges, unlike our friend's dog, Zack, who adores them. Some dogs have a lactose intolerance which makes it difficult for them to digest milk products, while other dogs can't get enough of the stuff. So the first time you try out a new food on your dog, keep the portion small and see what happens.

How many treats you give your dog depends on several factors. Your dog's age, size and level of activity are the obvious ones. Our dog gets two or three small biscuits daily and he usually gets some raw veggie slices when we're making our own dinner. On weekends he tends to get a lot more exercise so there are extra treats.

Finally, why make homemade treats for your dog? Why spend the afternoon turning ground-up chicken livers into hard brown biscuits that could only appeal to our canine friends? Why go to the store hunting for soy flour, liver powder and brewer's yeast when the market is filled with dozens of already prepared goodies for dogs? Will your dog be healthier . . . happier? Will his life be richer? We think so.

But there's another benefit to cooking for your pet. It's a way to connect with your dog and a time to focus on your special relationship.

3 GOING TO THE DOGS

Our Canine Consultants and Their Recipes

RUTHIE

RUTHIE

New York, New York

Ruthie may be an English springer spaniel, but she's pure New York. A street smart urban animal, she greets people with "high fives" and, if she knows you, "high tens." In love with the water, Ruthie swims the famous fountains of the city, and is partial to the one in front of the Metropolitan Museum of Art. As far as she is concerned, fountains are all decorative dog showers.

In New York, as in most cities, dog owners must clean up after their pets. Ruthie proudly carries her own newspaper for this purpose, clutching it in her mouth as her mother walks her down Park Avenue. Stodgy upper-east-side passersby mumble wisecracks like "Financial section?" as Ruthie searches for the perfect spot. When she drops the paper, you have arrived.

Ruthie's love of carrying things is true to her breed, but her sense of time and place is unique. This spaniel is very much a dog of the '90s. She rejects expensive label chew toys, is scornful of trendy lap dogs and ". . . will lift her nose and walk right past any pet wearing a sweater."

To reward Ruthie's sense of civic duty, we have developed these indigenous New York breakfast treats to go with her morning paper.

Ruthie's Breakfast Bagels . . .

Dog Bites!

RUTHIE'S
BREAKFAST BAGELS

Unlike the human variety, these little canine bagels are crunchy. To soften them, for the occasional treat of bagels with cream cheese or peanut butter, stick them in the microwave oven for about 30 seconds.

1 cup whole wheat or other whole grain flour
1 cup unbleached white flour
1 package yeast (¹/₄ ounce)
²/₃ cup chicken stock, warmed
1 tablespoon honey

Preheat the oven to 375 degrees.

In a large bowl combine the whole wheat flour with the yeast. Add the chicken stock and honey and beat for about 3 minutes. Gradually add the remaining flour. Knead the dough for a few minutes until smooth. Cover the dough and let it rest for about 5 minutes. Divide the dough into about 25 pieces, rolling each piece into a smooth ball. Punch a hole into each ball with your finger and gently pull the dough so the hole is about an inch wide. Don't be too fussy here, the little bagels rise into shape when they bake. Place all the bagels on a greased cookie sheet and allow to rise 5 minutes. Bake for 20 minutes. Turn the heat off and allow the bagels to cool in the oven.

PRISCILLA

Dog Bites!

PRISCILLA

Lyndhurst, New Jersey

Everyone has prejudices. This attractive terrier/poodle mix named Priscilla dislikes men. Her mother thinks she was mistreated by a mean man sometime in her past and by the time she and Priscilla were introduced at the Bergen County Pound, the dog had already made up her mind that men were no good.

Any time a man entered the house, Priscilla would growl continuously under her breath until he left. On one occasion, a plumber had the heel of his workboot bitten off when he failed to pick up on the animal's animosity and mistakenly turned his back on the dog.

When her mom's boyfriend moved in, Priscilla kept him under such constant surveillance that she hardly slept. He didn't like her much either and with good reason. The dog protested the interloper's presence by using the rug beside his bed as her bathroom. Every morning the poor man would march into the kitchen screaming the rhetorical question, "Who pooped on my rug?" at which time Priscilla would ". . . roll back her lips and snarl at him with such contempt" one would think he had done it!

The two are getting along much better now and Priscilla will only growl at him if he tries to pet her.

Since Priscilla loves olives, we created these little peace offerings to help reestablish her as "man's best friend."

Priscilla's Olive Branch Biscuits . . .

PRISCILLA'S OLIVE BRANCH BISCUITS

A first in biscuit diplomacy!

1 cup whole wheat flour
¹⁄₄ cup soy flour
¹⁄₄ cup brewer's yeast
¹⁄₂ teaspoon bone meal*
1 small clove garlic, minced
10 green olives, finely chopped
3 tablespoons olive oil
¹⁄₄ cup water

Preheat oven to 350 degrees.

Mix all the dry ingredients in a
medium-sized bowl. Toss in the garlic
and olives. Add the olive oil and the water
and mix well. Add more water if necessary. On a floured board, roll the dough
out to ¼" thickness and cut into desired shapes. Bake on an ungreased
cookie sheet for about 15 minutes, until golden brown. Store in an airtight
container in the refrigerator.

*Bone meal can be purchased at healthfood stores or pet supply stores. Use only
edible bone meal – not the garden variety.

GEORGE

GEORGE

Ridgewood, New Jersey

Before he was six months old, George already had a police record. George's misfortunes began when his open mouth bumped into an arm belonging to the neighbor's child, Jimmy.

"George didn't bite Jimmy — his mouth never closed," George's dad, a lawyer, explained. Jimmy's mother wasn't so sure and told the police so.

Being a Jack Russell terrier in suburbia can't be easy. With his hunting opportunities limited, George's build-up of energy must reach critical mass. To release pressure, George darts about until the inevitable accident lands him in the doghouse.

George is three years old now and has lived most of his life on probation. The pressure has left George with a permanent look of guilt, in spite of the fact that, except for occasional bouts of hyperactivity, his behavior has been exemplary. In exchange for aspiring to be a good dog, George requires bribes. The following recipe has been most successful in keeping George on the path of righteousness.

George's Tasty Bribes for Naughty Pups . . .

GEORGE'S TASTY BRIBES
FOR NAUGHTY PUPS

This treat might seem a bit extravagant but isn't your pooch worth it? Rich and chewy, this jerky is guaranteed to bring out the best in any dog.

1 flank steak (about 2 pounds)
¼ cup soy sauce
2 teaspoons honey
¼ teaspoon garlic powder
¼ teaspoon onion powder

Preheat the oven to 150 degrees or lowest setting.

Slice the steak, along the grain, into thin strips about 4" long. Slice each strip in half lengthwise (they should be about the width of chopsticks). Combine the remaining ingredients in a medium-sized bowl and mix well. Add the meat and toss until well coated. Marinate the meat about an hour.

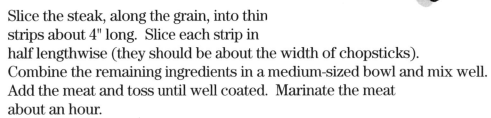

Cover two cookie sheets with aluminum foil and place the meat strips in a single layer without touching. Bake for about 7 hours until the meat is dry like jerky and dark in color. Store in an airtight container in the refrigerator or freeze for longer storage.

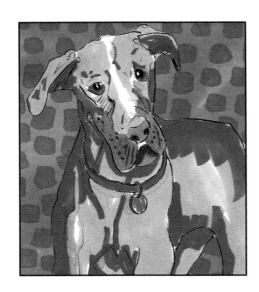

RODEO

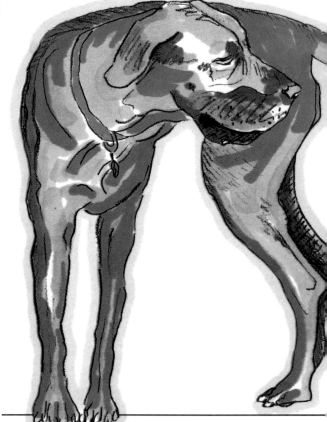

Dog Bites!

RODEO

Monticello, Florida

Rodeo is a great name and Rodeo is a Great Dane. She came to stay with her new family shortly after they were ". . . robbed for the last time." Isolated in the boondocks of central Florida, Rodeo's parents wanted a dog with a presence. And presence she had! By her first birthday Rodeo topped off at 120 pounds. Because of her size she always seemed closer than she was. The burglaries ceased — but so did the mail delivery, the milk delivery and the visits from Jehovah's Witnesses. A Federal Express man once got through to deliver a package, but he didn't wait for a signature.

Rodeo's mom affectionately describes her dog as "a schmoozer . . . a slobberer . . . all ears and paws and too many joints." Her huge tail sweeps away everything at coffee table height. In the dining room, Rodeo is not permitted to beg, but with all four feet on the floor, she will rest her enormous head on the tabletop and attempt to blend in with the place settings.

For all her size, Rodeo looks like a cartoon, as those who have gotten close enough are pleased to discover. Her ears, having never been docked, are floppy, and many have thought she resembles Mickey Mouse's dog, Pluto. Her best friend is a cat named Virgil; they are so close they eat from the same bowl. It's clear that with Rodeo one has "nothing to fear but fear itself."

Because of Rodeo's size, her recipe makes only one biscuit.

Rodeo's Big Barbecue Biscuit . . .

RODEO'S BIG BARBECUE BISCUIT

These hardy biscuits can be sized for any dog. Just be sure to adjust the baking time accordingly.

2 cups whole wheat flour
½ cup bulgur (cracked wheat)
2 tablespoons brewer's yeast
2 cloves garlic, minced
¼ cup vegetable oil
¾ cup beef stock
1 beaten egg
1 tablespoon Worcestershire sauce
1 tablespoon catsup

Preheat the oven to 350 degrees.

Combine in a large bowl the flour, bulgur, brewer's yeast and garlic. Add oil and stock and mix well. The dough should be quite stiff. Add water if dough is too dry.

In small bowl beat together the egg, Worcestershire sauce and the catsup.

Roll out to ¼" thickness, depending on the size of your dog. Cut into appropriate-sized biscuits and brush with egg mixture. Bake on ungreased cookie sheet for about 35 minutes. Turn heat off and let biscuits dry out in oven for several hours.

LILY

LILY

T hirteen years ago, Lily was one of those dogs featured by the local newspaper as "poster-dog-of-the-week." The reporter assigned to the column had gone to the pound to take the dog's mug shot for the paper and made the mistake of taking her home temporarily until someone adopted her. The newspaper was flooded with calls, but not in time. Lily had already adopted the reporter.

A dog of mixed inheritance, Lily is equal parts beagle, cocker spaniel and sheltie, making her somewhat confusing visually. Since she lacked a coherent image, her mother named her after Lillian Hellman in the hopes that she would ". . . grow up feisty . . . stand up for herself . . . and be her own dog." Lily did all that and more.

According to Lily's mom, you could search the world in vain for a more compassionate creature. If she's present during a terrible argument, Lily will immediately identify the injured party, jump onto his or her lap and tremble violently until the person feels better.

Lily's faults are excessively loud snoring, snarling at potential house buyers (journalists move a lot), and requiring a small dog biscuit to be placed on top of her dinner before she will eat it; all minor transgressions by anyone's standards.

We created this first course to jump start Lily's appetite.

Lily's Silly Appetizers . . .

Dog Bites!

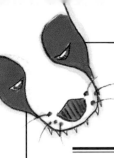

LILY'S SILLY APPETIZERS

Ground turkey works just as well as the ground beef. The size of the meatballs can be varied according to the size of your dog. Serve these at room temperature or slightly warmed in the microwave.

½ pound ground beef
1 small carrot, finely grated
1 tablespoon grated cheese
½ teaspoon garlic powder
½ cup whole wheat bread crumbs
1 egg, beaten
1 tablespoon tomato paste

Preheat the oven to 350 degrees.

In a medium-sized bowl, combine ground beef, carrot, cheese, garlic powder and bread crumbs. Add the egg and tomato paste and mix well.

Using your hands, roll the mixture into marble-sized meatballs and place on a lightly greased cookie sheet. Bake for about 15 minutes until the meatballs are brown and firm. Cool the meatballs completely before storing in an airtight container in the refrigerator. These freeze well.

BON-BON

Dog Bites!

BON-BON

Chappaqua, New York

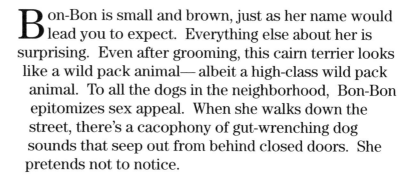

Bon-Bon is small and brown, just as her name would lead you to expect. Everything else about her is surprising. Even after grooming, this cairn terrier looks like a wild pack animal— albeit a high-class wild pack animal. To all the dogs in the neighborhood, Bon-Bon epitomizes sex appeal. When she walks down the street, there's a cacophony of gut-wrenching dog sounds that seep out from behind closed doors. She pretends not to notice.

From a human perspective, Bon-Bon is a little overanxious in pursuing her canine relationships. She has trouble expressing her love in a nonviolent way. When her heart is in the right place, her teeth aren't.

People, on the other hand, she has down to a science, especially when it comes to securing treats. Early on, Bon-Bon developed a "deserving look" irresistible to all but the most callous of individuals. And while her technique is transparent, it works every time.

Bon-Bon's Just Desserts for Deserving Dogs . . .

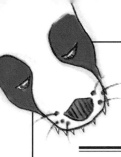

BON-BON'S JUST DESSERTS FOR DESERVING DOGS

Bon-Bon, like most dogs we know, has a sweet tooth. This delicious, spicy and slightly sweet dessert is just right to finish off her dinner. Dogs aren't as vulnerable to tooth decay as we are. Sweet treats, however, should not be allowed to ruin their appetites for more nutritious foods.

1 cup whole wheat flour
¼ cup wheat germ
1 teaspoon ginger
½ teaspoon cinnamon
2 tablespoons honey
2 tablespoons molasses
2 tablespoons safflower oil
1 egg yolk

Preheat oven to 350 degrees.

In a medium-sized bowl mix together the flour, wheat germ, and spices. In a small bowl combine the honey, molasses, oil and egg yolk. Mix well and add to the flour mixture. Knead dough briefly.

Roll out to ¼" thick and cut with cookie cutters. Bake on ungreased cookie sheet 15 minutes, until lightly browned. Turn off heat and let the cookies dry out in oven until completely cooled and quite hard. Store in airtight container.

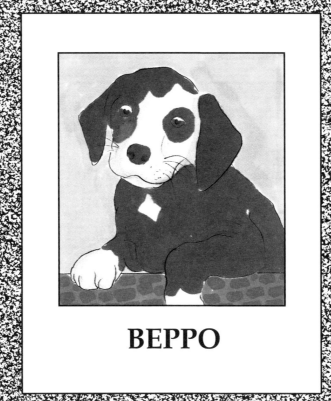

BEPPO

BEPPO

Great Neck, Long Island

Ogden Nash once wrote "A door is what a dog is perpetually on the wrong side of." He could have had Beppo in mind. An escape artist, Beppo could turn doorknobs and lift latches. He could tunnel under fences or hurdle them. It was expensive bailing Beppo out of the pound every time he was caught by the local dogcatcher.

In desperation, Beppo's family set up a dog trolley in the backyard. The next day Beppo was found three miles away dragging several feet of frayed rope. Short of putting the dog in leg irons, there was nothing left to do. After some thought, a stakeout was planned in the hope of learning the dog's technique. Hiding in the bushes, Beppo's dad watched as the dog, attached to the trolley, taxied down to the end of his runway, turned and ran full speed to the opposite end. As the line went taut, Beppo went ballistic, his body snapping around and "cracking the whip." In an instant, the rope exploded to smithereens and Beppo tumbled to a halt. Then without fanfare, he got up and left.

When the pound called, Beppo's dad was already looking for his checkbook. Gradually, anger gave way to resignation. After all, the dog was damn good at what he did.

For some unknown reason, Beppo remained homebound for the next five years. Then one day his wanderlust got the better of him and he disappeared again, this time for good.

In memory of this clever little traveler, we have developed these tasty treats for the road.

Beppo's Treats to Go . . .

Dog Bites!

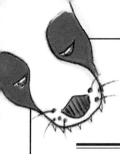

BEPPO'S TREATS
TO GO

Dogs love peanut butter! These high protein biscuits are terrific for any dog on the go. As an extra special treat, make a sandwich cookie by spreading some peanut butter and a drop of honey between two biscuits.

3 cups whole wheat flour
½ cup rolled oats
2 teaspoons baking powder
1 ½ cups milk
1 ¼ cups peanut butter
1 tablespoon molasses

Preheat the oven to 350 degrees.

Combine the flour, oats and baking powder in a large bowl. Using a food processor or blender, mix the milk, peanut butter and molasses until smooth and add to dry ingredients. Using your hands, knead the ingredients together. Dough will be quite stiff.

Roll the dough out to ¼" thickness and cut with cookie cutters. Bake for about 20 minutes or until lightly browned. Turn off the heat and leave the biscuits in the oven until cool. Store in airtight container.

TESS

Dog Bites!

TESS

Clove Valley, New York

Tess will herd anything that moves. In this Australian shepherd's mind, deer, woodchucks, rabbits, moths, cars and people all need to be organized into ever-tightening circles. Tess will even herd her own shadow which, under her careful guidance, never strays.

Not everyone likes to be herded, especially the patients who seek spinal realignment from Tess's mother, a chiropractor. But with her good looks, Tess is more marveled at than maligned. Her brown, white and black markings are almost painterly and wouldn't be out of place on a canvas. She is a masterpiece of design.

Second only to her beauty is her gentle, loving disposition. Tess is a sheep in wolf's clothing. You get the feeling shortly after being introduced to Tess that her kissing is genuine, unconditional and uncontrollable.

One can't help but feel the need to reciprocate. Here's a treat that makes mutual adoration easier.

Tess's Nice Breath Biscuits . . .

TESS'S NICE BREATH BISCUITS

Feed these green, specked treats to your dog and notice the difference! Mint and parsley are natural breath fresheners. The crunchy biscuits prevent tartar from building up on your dog's teeth. While we're on the subject, most vets recommend cleaning your dog's teeth regularly. We use baking soda with a little salt and a soft child's toothbrush. Bo puts up with it and his teeth are shiny and white.

2 cups whole wheat flour
¹/₂ cup cornmeal
¹/₃ cup chopped fresh mint (or 1 tablespoon dried)
¹/₂ cup chopped parsley
6 tablespoons safflower oil (¼c)
³/₄ cup water

Preheat oven to 350 degrees.

Combine flour, cornmeal, mint and parsley in a large bowl. Add oil and water and mix thoroughly.

Roll out to ¼" on floured surface and cut with cookie cutters.

Bake for 40 minutes, or until lightly browned. Turn heat off and let biscuits dry out in oven for several hours. Store in refrigerator in airtight container.

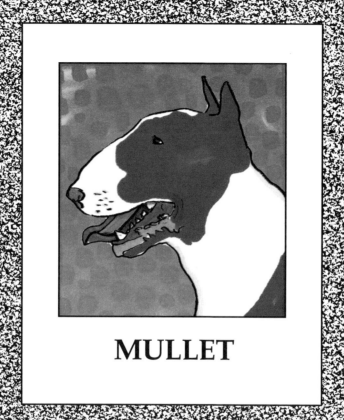

MULLET

MULLET

Mullet is a dog of the sea. He lives and works on the fishing boat *Mudshark*, berthed in Ponce Inlet. Mullet himself was birthed inland and originally named "Bullet." But like many dogs of bull terrier extraction, Bullet ended up at the pound where his current owner, Captain John, picked him up for ten dollars and changed his name to the more appropriate "Mullet."

Mullet has proven to be worth every penny Captain John paid for him. Up on the bow, Mullet has an uncanny ability to find the birds who in turn spot the fish. When Mullet points his nose to the starboard, Captain John turns the wheel until the ship's nose and the dog's nose line up. "By God, I can turn off the sonar fish finder when he's on," claims the captain.

Dockside, Mullet is invaluable in guarding the *Mudshark* when the captain goes to town. One unfortunate thief had the seat of his trousers torn off when he was caught red-handed by the good dog. The blood-stained seat of his pants still flies from the gin pole of the *Mudshark* as a reminder to all those who would dare board uninvited.

For all he does, we feel this salty dog deserves a special treat.

Mullet's Marvelous Mackerel Morsels . . .

Dog Bites!

MULLET'S MARVELOUS MACKEREL MORSELS

Canned mackerel is a great bargain. Mackerel is a wonderful source of protein as well as calcium since it is usually canned with the bones included. The bones are very soft, so there is no risk of your dog choking on them.

1 can mackerel (15 ounces)
½ cup whole grain bread crumbs
1 tablespoon minced onion, optional
1 tablespoon minced green pepper
2 tablespoons vegetable oil
1 egg, beaten

Preheat oven to 350 degrees.

Using a fork, mash the mackerel in a medium-sized bowl. Add the remaining ingredients and mix well. Using your hands, roll the dough into walnut-sized balls. Press to flatten them slightly and bake on a greased cookie sheet for about 20 minutes. They should be firm and lightly browned. Flip the fish cakes and put them back in the oven for about 5 minutes to dry them out slightly. Cool completely before storing in an airtight container in the refrigerator.

SPECK

SPECK

New York, New York

Speck was supposed to have been a ten-week-old beagle puppy. At least that's what the man at the pound claimed. After a year Speck hadn't grown an ounce. At four pounds, either Speck was the smallest beagle on record or she was not a beagle.

When the answer finally came, it was such a relief. A veterinarian finally diagnosed Speck as being a healthy Chihuahua/terrier mix and very much full-grown. "A large weight lifted from our shoulders," exclaimed Speck's parents. "We thought we were doing something wrong." After months of force-feeding and stretching exercises, life for Speck could now get back to normal.

As a result of her parents' overcompensating, Speck refuses to believe her true identity and still thinks she's a growing beagle. But since her mouth is not any bigger than her stomach, her treats have to be kept in scale.

Speck's Tempting Tidbits for Lap Dogs . . .

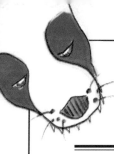

SPECK'S TEMPTING TIDBITS FOR LAP DOGS

These special treats will be gratefully gobbled up by any size dog. Buy the leanest ground beef you can find. With less fat, the treats will be healthier for your dog and stay fresher longer.

1 pound extra lean ground beef
3 tablespoons soy sauce
¼ teaspoon garlic powder
¼ teaspoon ground ginger
¼ teaspoon ground pepper
¼ teaspoon ground cloves

Preheat oven to 150 degrees or the lowest setting.

Combine all ingredients in a bowl and mix well.

Line a four-sided cookie sheet with aluminum foil.

Spread meat mixture on cookie sheet and flatten with your hands or rolling pin to ¼" thick. Place meat in preheated oven. Prop oven door open a crack using a wooden spoon so moisture can escape. Bake for two hours.

Remove meat from oven and blot with paper towel to remove excess fat. Cut into squares and invert onto clean cookie sheet. Return to oven for another two hours until meat is dry like jerky. Cool to room temperature and store in airtight container in the refrigerator—or freeze for longer storage.

ORSO

ORSO

Turner, Maine

Orso is the consummate golden retriever. He will drop a soggy tennis ball in your lap so many times you will have to change your pants before breakfast. If you make the mistake of throwing the ball, you're his for the day.

Italian for "bear," the name Orso is perfect for this large, handsome animal. Orso is not a gourmet. He even ate a beer can once. But if you could pin him down, the number one item on Orso's short list would be liver. To Orso, joy and liver are synonymous.

Being a Maine dog has advantages: summers are spent running through fields and swimming in ponds, and the formidable winters are spent shivering. So Orso has an easier time burning up calories than his more sedentary urban cousins. Several snacks a day are allowed and are lovingly appreciated.

Orso's Real Good Liver Slivers . . .

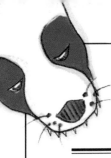

ORSO'S REAL GOOD LIVER SLIVERS

Any dog fond of liver (and what dog isn't?) will devour these iron-rich, crunchy biscuits.

½ pound cooked chicken livers
1 cup chicken stock
½ cup corn oil
1 tablespoon chopped parsley
1 cup dry milk
1 cup rolled oats

½ cup brewer's yeast
1 cup soy flour
1 cup cornmeal
3 cups whole wheat flour

Preheat oven to 350 degrees.

In food processor or blender, process chicken livers, chicken stock, corn oil and parsley until smooth. Transfer to large bowl. Add dry milk, rolled oats, brewer's yeast, soy flour and cornmeal. Mix well. Gradually add whole wheat flour. You'll have to use your hands here, kneading in as much of the flour as it takes to create a very stiff dough.

Roll dough out to ¼" thick and cut into stick shapes, about ½" by 4" (depending on the size of your dog).

Bake on ungreased cookie sheet for 20 to 25 minutes until lightly browned and crisp. Turn off heat and let biscuits dry out in oven for several hours. Store in the refrigerator.

B.J.

B.J.

Long Island, New York

B.J. is all hair and air. When he dives into the family pool for his daily swim, B.J. goes in a Bichon Frise and comes out an X-ray of his former self. Suddenly he looks his mere seventeen pounds. In spite of his love of the water, B.J. will not go outside if it's raining. He once waited twenty hours to avoid getting his feet wet. When the rain stopped, he ran out and jumped back into the pool.

B.J. is a well-heeled dog with a first-rate grooming salon, "Just Paws." B.J. deserves a quality coiffeur because, as far as he is concerned, he is not a dog at all. Whenever he sits on the furniture, he sits like a human, with his front paws up, looking something like a trained bear. He has been known to stay in this position through an entire opera, which his dad swears is the dog's favorite music.

B.J.'s prize possession, in fact his only possession, is a small, wet, thoroughly chewed stuffed dog. He sleeps with it, cuddles and otherwise loves it to pieces and sees no apparent contradiction in giving it "a little death shake" from time to time.

Finally, B.J. is a dog for all seasons. After a winter blizzard, B.J. "will run out in the yard, flip over on his back and make angels in the snow." Then he scampers back into the house and melts for several hours.

Every year on his birthday, B.J. gets all of his favorite foods: barbecued chicken, pizza and this frozen goodie.

B.J.'s Peanutty Pupcicles . . .

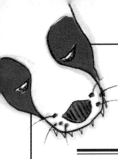

B.J.'S PEANUTTY PUPCICLES

Our dog loves ice cubes, frozen peas, and frozen bananas. These little "pupcicles" are easy to make and have been a hit with all our pup "tasters."

1 ripe banana
¹/₂ cup peanut butter
¹/₄ cup wheat germ
¹/₄ cup chopped unsalted peanuts

In a small bowl, mash banana and peanut butter together using a fork. Mix in wheat germ. Place in refrigerator for about an hour until firm.

With your hands, roll rounded teaspoonfuls of mixture into balls. Roll balls in peanuts, coating them evenly. Place on cookie sheet in freezer. When completely frozen, pack into airtight containers and store in freezer.

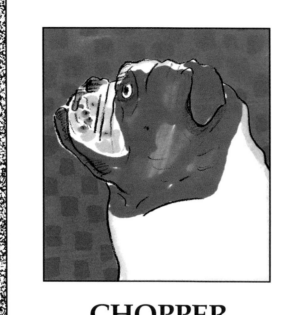

CHOPPER

CHOPPER

Richmond, Vermont

If you could sculpt a dog out of a knot of muscle you would end up with Chopper. Except for a few wrinkles around the face and neck, there are no wasted lines on this bulldog. Chopper's owner affectionately refers to him as a "walking cramp." He is a dog who is genetically locked into a state of readiness. Even his tail has a hard time relaxing and appears to be screwed into his body.

Winston Churchill once quipped, "The nose of the bulldog has been slanted backward so that he can breathe without letting go." This makes good sense given the fact that aerodynamics could not be that important to any breed with a square head.

Chopper's reputation for dogged persistence and endurance is legendary in this small northern Vermont town, where for eight months of the year "it's colder than a well-digger's knees." His dad will proudly tell you about the time Chopper escaped from the yard by pulling at his chain so many times that the links, each as big around as your pinky, gradually separated.

Despite this formidable talent, Chopper is as gentle and affectionate as any dog you have ever known, which seems even more ingratiating given what he could do to you if he wanted to. How do the neighbors feel about Chopper's pleasing disposition? "Grateful!"

Chopper's One Tough Cookie for One Tough Dog . . .

CHOPPER'S ONE TOUGH COOKIE FOR ONE TOUGH DOG

These spicy biscuits are the doggie equivalent of "jaw breakers." Big dogs will enjoy the challenge and all that crunching will be good for their teeth and gums.

3½ cups rye flour
¾ cup nonfat dry milk powder
1 tablespoon garlic powder
1 tablespoon onion powder
1 tablespoon liver powder

1 teaspoon bone meal*
2 tablespoons chopped parsley
⅓ cup vegetable oil
¾ cup water
1 egg, beaten

Preheat the oven to 325 degrees.

In a large bowl, combine all the dry ingredients. Add the oil, water and egg and mix well. This dough is tough, so use your hands! On a floured board, roll the dough out to ¼" thickness and cut into large bone shapes. Bake in the oven for 25 minutes. Check the biscuits frequently to make sure they're not burning. Turn off the heat and leave the biscuits in the oven overnight to dry out. Store in an airtight container in the refrigerator.

*Bone meal can be purchased at healthfood stores or pet supply stores. Use only edible bone meal — not the garden variety.

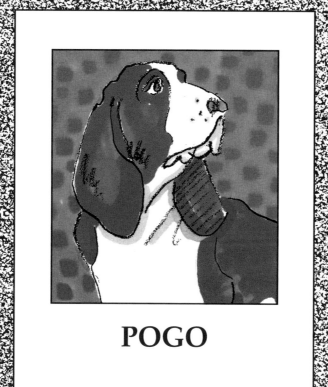

POGO

Dog Bites!

POGO

Birmingham, Michigan

Everything on Pogo droops. Pogo has fought gravity and lost. If only his legs were longer or closer together, ground clearance wouldn't be so critical. But long legs and a short wheelbase are not part of a basset hound's design.

Compounding the problem, Pogo loves to eat out, consuming a majority of his calories away from home. No one knows where he finds these extra meals and to make matters worse, there seems to be a code of silence among the neighbors. The little kids in the area have a song they sing when they see Pogo:

"He's the tubby puppers 'cause he eats too many suppers."

Pogo's life would have been a drag both figuratively and literally were it not for his caring owner, who created this special diet snack. Designed to keep Pogo close to home and high off the ground, this recipe tastes great and is more filling.

Pogo's Light Biscuits for Belly Draggers . . .

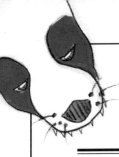

POGO'S LIGHT BISCUITS FOR BELLY DRAGGERS

Delicious and power-packed, these treats will fill them up without filling them out.

2 cups whole wheat flour
½ cup soy flour
½ cup cornmeal
¼ cup brewer's yeast
¼ cup dry milk
1 teaspoon garlic powder

1 tablespoon finely chopped fresh parsley
1 package dry active yeast
¼ cup warm water
1 cup chicken stock
1 beaten egg mixed with
 1 tablespoon milk

Preheat the oven to 300 degrees.

Combine the flours, cornmeal, brewer's yeast, dry milk, garlic powder and parsley in large bowl. In a small bowl dissolve the yeast in warm water. Stir well and add the chicken stock.

Pour the liquid mixture into dry ingredients. Working with your hands, combine all the ingredients completely. Knead for several minutes.

Sprinkle a board with additional cornmeal and roll the dough out to ¼" thickness. Cut into dog bone shapes and place on an ungreased cookie sheet. Brush lightly with egg glaze and bake for 45 minutes. Turn heat off and let the biscuits dry out in oven for several hours or overnight. Store in airtight container.

TOOTSIE

TOOTSIE

Chappaqua, New York

When Tootsie's mom went looking for a puppy, she wisely left her money and checkbook at home. She was not going to buy a dog on impulse. But the instant she set eyes on Tootsie, she drove home for her wallet so fast she hardly noticed the flashing lights of the police car behind her. After hearing the excuse, the good policeman let her go.

Tootsie is irresistible. At barely six pounds, she is small even for a Shih Tzu. True to her astrological sign, Aries, Tootsie is extremely demanding of her mother and insists on doing everything with her.

Tootsie sits on the sink when her mom puts on makeup in the morning. Then Tootsie goes to work, charming all the customers who buy their coffee and muffins at her mother's "Cafe La Track" in the town's train station. Tootsie even sits on her mom's shoulder looking out the windshield during weekend car trips to Ithaca, logging four hours each way. And at night Tootsie sleeps under the covers.

Inseparable, Tootsie and her mom also dine together. A dog of many tastes, Tootsie likes carrots, mangos and tomatoes in addition to her kibble. For this loving little dog we have worked up this tomatoey treat.

Tootsie's Marinara Munchie . . .

Dog Bites!

TOOTSIE'S MARINARA MUNCHIE

These bite-sized pizza treats are perfect for the most demanding of dogs!

1 cup unbleached flour
1 cup cornmeal
¼ cup brewer's yeast
½ teaspoon garlic powder
½ teaspoon dried oregano
½ teaspoon dried basil

½ cup grated Romano cheese
3 tablespoons olive oil
1 tablespoon tomato paste
½ cup water
1 egg beaten with 1 tablespoon
*   tomato paste*

Preheat oven to 350 degrees.

In large bowl, combine flour, cornmeal, brewer's yeast, garlic powder, oregano, basil and grated cheese and mix well. Add olive oil, tomato paste and water and mix thoroughly.

Dust board with cornmeal and roll the dough out to ¼" thick. Cut into 3" circles and brush each circle lightly with the tomato and egg topping. Using a sharp knife or pizza wheel, cut each circle into four wedges. Place on ungreased cookie sheet and bake for 25 minutes. Turn heat off and allow biscuits to cool in oven. Store in airtight container in the refrigerator.

COCOA

COCOA

South Orange, New Jersey

C ocoa was a "special" at the local animal shelter and special he was. Of uncertain parentage, Cocoa had signs of Airedale, Labrador retriever and a dash of German shepherd in him. At eight weeks, Cocoa looked like a cocoa bean, hence his name.

On Cocoa's first birthday, his dad, proud as a peacock over the dog, went out and bought him The Super Deluxe Log Cabin Doghouse Kit and spent the next month of Sundays putting it together: "Cocoa didn't love it." Worse yet, he wouldn't even go in it. His dad put food inside. It rotted. He tried pushing the dog in, but after each attempt, only skid marks remained. In desperation, he even got down on all fours and crawled in to show Cocoa how cozy it was. That was a mistake! Backing out, his trousers caught on a splinter and he departed the doghouse with considerably less than he went in with. It was at that moment that Cocoa's dad got a hold of himself. After all, the doghouse was a present and the dog could do with it what he wanted.

Cocoa now spends his days sleeping beside the doghouse. Even in a thunder shower, Cocoa sleeps beside the doghouse. If another dog tries to go in, Cocoa growls. It's his.

We were intrigued by this happy camper, so we created a snack just for him.

Cocoa's Picnic Snack . . .

COCOA'S PICNIC SNACK

Chocolate contains a substance that is toxic to dogs. Carob, available in health food stores, is a tasty substitute and provides calcium and fiber.

2 cups whole wheat flour
¼ cup carob powder
1 teaspoon bone meal*
1 egg, beaten
2 tablespoons vegetable oil
1 tablespoon honey
⅓ cup milk
cornmeal

Preheat the oven to 350 degrees.

In a large bowl, combine the flour, carob powder and bone meal. Add the remaining ingredients (except for the cornmeal) and mix well. Sprinkle a board with cornmeal and roll dough out to ¼" thickness. Cut into shapes using cookie cutters, about 1" in diameter. Bake on an ungreased cookie sheet for about 20 minutes. Turn heat off and allow cookies to cool in the oven. Store in airtight container.

*Bone meal can be purchased at healthfood stores or pet supply stores. Use only edible bone meal — not the garden variety.

THURBER

THURBER

Brooklyn, New York

Thurber is the Don Juan of dogs. A cocker spaniel with a stylish Mohawk haircut, Thurber's carnal interest peaked right at the time he was "fixed." From then on, his imagination took over and he saw love objects everywhere he looked. Nothing was too abstract. Thurber would mount dogs, cats, statues and legs of all descriptions; he even climbed aboard a topiary sheep at a nearby botanical garden. And when Thurber embraced, there was no letting go.

Thurber's parents panicked and took him to the vet. Before the vet could get a firm grip on the situation, Thurber beat him to it. When the good doctor regained use of his leg and his composure, it was agreed that therapy was in order. A specialist was called in.

Using patience and a rolled-up newspaper, the psychotherapist impressed on Thurber that he didn't need to get a leg up on everyone and that his social climbing was, in fact, antisocial. Now, except for an occasional mistake, Thurber's relationships are platonic and his life more spiritual.

These crunchy little heart-shaped biscuits have helped to deliver Thurber from temptation.

Thurber's Little Passion Patties . . .

THURBER'S LITTLE PASSION PATTIES

These honey-flavored hearts are the perfect love substitute for the animal in your animal.

1 ½ cups barley flour
½ cup soy flour
2 teaspoons baking powder
½ cup dried currants
⅔ cup milk
1 tablespoon honey
2 tablespoons safflower oil

Preheat oven to 300 degrees.

Combine the flours, baking
powder and currants in a medium-sized bowl. Stir in the milk, honey and oil.
Mix well.

On a floured board, roll the dough out to ¼" thickness and cut with a
heart-shaped cookie cutter. Bake on a lightly greased cookie sheet for about
20 minutes until lightly browned. Turn the heat off and leave the cookies in
the oven until cool. Store in an airtight container in the refrigerator.

PAVLOV

Dog Bites!

PAVLOV

Homestead, Florida

P avlov is exquisitely suited for life in the far north. A Siberian husky, his coat is a marvel of heat conservation, enabling him to sleep outdoors at 40 degrees below zero. Regrettably, Pavlov has never even seen snow, let alone 40 below. Most of his life has been spent in the sub-tropical Everglades of Florida. His dad, a pastor at a local church in Nome, Alaska, was transferred to Homestead, Florida, shortly after adopting Pavlov. The clergyman considered leaving Pavlov behind but it was too late. They had bonded.

Ordinarily, we would have disqualified the tropical husky as a poor geographic match were it not for this mitigating factor—Pavlov lives in an air-conditioned doghouse when he's not out chasing alligators.

When the good pastor tolls the dinner bell, salivation is near!

Pavlov's Mouth-Watering Treats . . .

PAVLOV'S MOUTH-WATERING TREATS

These bite-sized cheesy goodies will make any dog's mouth water. It's also a great recipe for using up leftovers!

2 eggs, beaten
1 cup grated cheese
1 cup cooked rice or bulgur
1 cup cooked vegetables, chopped ,
  grated or mashed (carrots, potatoes,
  zucchini, peas, etc.)
1 tablespoon chopped parsley, optional
1 tablespoon brewer's yeast

Preheat the oven to 350 degrees.

Mix all the ingredients well. Drop by teaspoonfuls onto a greased cookie sheet. Bake for about 12 minutes or until set and lightly browned. Cool and store in an airtight container in the refrigerator.

BO

BO

Chappaqua, New York

Of all the commands Bo learned in puppy obedience class, the only one he unfailingly obeys is "Sit."

Bo retained "Stay," "Heel," and "Come," only long enough to receive his diploma. But "Sit" he does well. Bo will "Sit" on command at 150 yards' distance. Bo will "Sit" in a puddle. Bo will "Sit" in a dogfight. Bo will "Sit" in the middle of chasing a squirrel.

In spite of his training lapses, Bo is the best dog we've ever had. He's affectionate, forgiving, funny and his fur feels nice. In a tug-of-war Bo won't let go. He will fall asleep, but he won't let go. Bo is a perfect creature.

Eventually he taught us to "Stay" when he didn't want us to leave and to "Come" when he needed us. Together we manage.

Bo's Little Carrot Cakes . . .

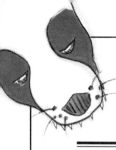

BO'S LITTLE CARROT CAKES

Bo loves carrots. He loves them whole, grated, chopped, in salads, sprinkled over kibble and baked in these wholesome little muffins. Feel free to replace the carrots with your dog's favorite fruit or veggie, such as zucchini or apples. For small dogs, try baking these in appetizer-sized muffin tins. Regular muffin tins work well for larger dogs.

1 ½ cups whole wheat flour
1 cup rolled oats
1 cup oat bran
1 teaspoon baking soda
1 teaspoon cinnamon
2 cups grated carrots

½ cup sunflower seeds
1 egg
¼ cup maple syrup or honey
3 tablespoons corn oil
1 cup milk

Preheat oven to 375 degrees.

Combine flour, oats, oat bran, baking soda, cinnamon, carrots and sunflower seeds in large bowl. In small bowl beat together egg, maple syrup, corn oil and milk. Pour egg mixture into dry ingredients and mix well.

Bake in lightly greased muffin tins. Small muffins will take 15 to 20 minutes and larger muffins will take 25 to 30 minutes. When a cake tester comes out clean, turn heat off and leave muffins in oven until completely cool. Store in airtight container in refrigerator.

4 PARTY ANIMAL

Special Treats for Special Occasions

"Every dog has his day," wrote Miguel De Cervantes in the sixteenth century. When that day comes, we humans should be prepared with special treats to mark the occasion. Birthdays, religious holidays like Christmas and Hanukkah, Thanksgiving and even Valentine's Day are fine times to reflect on our canine relationships.

There is something perfect about gathering together with our dogs, our children and in some cases our relatives for the purpose of connecting, cuddling and overeating. The following are recipes for unleashing our feelings at holiday time.

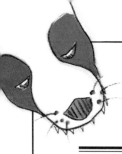

BOWZER'S BIRTHDAY CAKES

Liver Cupcakes

2 cups whole wheat flour
2 tablespoons liver powder
2 teaspoons baking powder

⅓ cup vegetable oil
1 egg, beaten
1 cup beef stock

Preheat the oven to 350 degrees.

In a bowl, combine flour, liver powder and baking powder. Add the remaining ingredients and mix well. Grease muffin tins (regular size for big dogs or appetizer size for little dogs) and spoon in the batter, filling them two-thirds full. Bake the cupcakes 15 minutes for the small cupcakes and 25 minutes for the large. Cool completely before frosting. Decorate each cupcake with a small dog biscuit (Cocoa's Picnic Snacks are a terrific garnish).

Peanut Butter Frosting

¼ cup smooth peanut butter
½ cup whipped cream cheese

In a small bowl, beat the peanut butter and cream cheese together until they're light and fluffy.

HOLIDAY
PUP TARTS

Peanut Butter Tarts

Use recipe for Cocoa's Picnic Snacks (Carob Cookies)
chunky peanut butter

Preheat the oven to 350 degrees.

Roll dough out as recipe indicates. Grease tiny tart
molds or muffin tins and line them with the carob
dough as if making a pie crust. Bake them for about
12 minutes. Cool completely and carefully remove
from the molds. Fill each carob cup with a dollop
of peanut butter.

Little Apple Tarts

Use recipe for Beppo's Treats to Go (Peanut Butter Biscuits)
unsweetened apple sauce

Preheat the oven to 350 degrees.

Roll out dough as indicated in the recipe. Grease tiny tart molds or muffin tins and line them
with the dough as if making a pie crust. Bake them for about 12 minutes. Cool completely
and remove from the molds. Fill each peanut butter cup with a dollop of apple sauce.

5 LAST LICKS

Some Final Thoughts

By now you and your dog have shared your affection for one another. You've broken biscuit together. And you've both tasted what it's like to connect with a creature so different it could have easily come from another planet, yet so similar it could be an extension of yourself.

In this age of confused values, where time equals money, we forget that it's "time" itself that's important. The time we share.

We close with this quote.

> **"My little old dog:**
> **A heart beat at my feet."**
>
> **—Edith Wharton**